The Distances

Poems by
Charles Olson

grove press, inc. / new york

evergreen books ltd. / london

Many of these poems were first published by: *Ark II / Moby I, Artisan, Black Mountain Review, Cendre, Evergreen Review, Fragmente,* Jargon Press, *Measure, Montevallo Review,* New Directions, *Origin, Partisan Review, Shigaku, Vou, Western Review* and *Yugen*

CONTENTS

THE KINGFISHERS

1

What does not change / is the will to change

He woke, fully clothed, in his bed. He
remembered only one thing, the birds, how
when he came in, he had gone around the rooms
and got them back in their cage, the green one first,
she with the bad leg, and then the blue,
the one they had hoped was a male

Otherwise? Yes, Fernand, who had talked lispingly of Albers & Angkor Vat.
He had left the party without a word. How he got up, got into his coat,
I do not know. When I saw him, he was at the door, but it did not matter,
he was already sliding along the wall of the night, losing himself
in some crack of the ruins. That it should have been he who said, "The kingfishers!
who cares
for their feathers
now?"

His last words had been, "The pool is slime." Suddenly everyone,
ceasing their talk, sat in a row around him, watched
they did not so much hear, or pay attention, they
wondered, looked at each other, smirked, but listened,
he repeated and repeated, could not go beyond his thought
"The pool   the kingfishers' feathers were wealth   why
did the export stop?"

It was then he left

2

I thought of the E on the stone, and of what Mao said
la lumiere"
              but the kingfisher
de l'aurore"
              but the kingfisher flew west
est devant nous!
             he got the color of his breast
             from the heat of the setting sun!

The features are, the feebleness of the feet (syndactylism of the 3rd & 4th digit)
the bill, serrated, sometimes a pronounced beak, the wings
where the color is, short and round, the tail
inconspicuous.

But not these things were the factors. Not the birds.
The legends are
legends. Dead, hung up indoors, the kingfisher
will not indicate a favoring wind,
or avert the thunderbolt. Nor, by its nesting,
still the waters, with the new year, for seven days.
It is true, it does nest with the opening year, but not on the waters.
It nests at the end of a tunnel bored by itself in a bank. There,
six or eight white and translucent eggs are laid, on fishbones
not on bare clay, on bones thrown up in pellets by the birds.

                    On these rejectamenta
(as they accumulate they form a cup-shaped structure) the young are born.
And, as they are fed and grow, this nest of excrement and decayed fish becomes
                    a dripping, fetid mass

Mao concluded:
             nous devons
                   nous lever
                            et agir!

3

When the attentions change / the jungle
leaps in
            even the stones are split
                        they rive

Or,
enter
that other conqueror we more naturally recognize
he so resembles ourselves

But the E
cut so rudely on that oldest stone
sounded otherwise,
was differently heard

as, in another time, were treasures used:

(and, later, much later, a fine ear thought
a scarlet coat)

            "of green feathers   feet, beaks and eyes
            of gold

            "animals likewise,
            resembling snails

            "a large wheel, gold, with figures of unknown four-foots,
            and worked with tufts of leaves, weight
            3800 ounces

            "last, two birds, of thread and featherwork, the quills
            gold, the feet
            gold, the two birds perched on two reeds
            gold, the reeds arising from two embroidered mounds,
            one yellow, the other
            white.

"And from each reed hung
seven feathered tassels.

In this instance, the priests
(in dark cotton robes, and dirty,
their dishevelled hair matted with blood, and flowing wildly
over their shoulders)
rush in among the people, calling on them
to protect their gods

And all now is war
where so lately there was peace,
and the sweet brotherhood, the use
of tilled fields.

4

Not one death but many,
not accumulation but change, the feed-back proves, the feed-back is
the law

      Into the same river no man steps twice
      When fire dies air dies
      No one remains, nor is, one

Around an appearance, one common model, we grow up
many. Else how is it,
if we remain the same,
we take pleasure now
in what we did not take pleasure before? love
contrary objects? admire and/or find fault? use
other words, feel other passions, have
nor figure, appearance, disposition, tissue
the same?

      To be in different states without a change
      is not a possibility

We can be precise. The factors are
in the animal and/or the machine the factors are
communication and/or control, both involve
the message. And what is the message? The message is
a discrete or continuous sequence of measurable events distributed in time

is the birth of air, is
the birth of water, is
a state between
the origin and
the end, between
birth and the beginning of
another fetid nest

is change, presents
no more than itself

And the too strong grasping of it,
when it is pressed together and condensed,
loses it

This very thing you are

II

They buried their dead in a sitting posture
serpent   cane   razor   ray of the sun

And she sprinkled water on the head of the child, crying
"Cioa-coatl! Cioa-coatl!"
with her face to the west

Where the bones are found, in each personal heap
with what each enjoyed, there is always
the Mongolian louse

The light is in the east. Yes. And we must rise, act. Yet
in the west, despite the apparent darkness (the whiteness
which covers all), if you look, if you can bear, if you can, long enough

as long as it was necessary for him, my guide
to look into the yellow of that longest-lasting rose

so you must, and, in that whiteness, into that face, with what candor, look

and, considering the dryness of the place
　　　the long absence of an adequate race

　　　　　(of the two who first came, each a conquistador, one healed, the other
　　　　　tore the eastern idols down, toppled
　　　　　the temple walls, which, says the excuser
　　　　　were black from human gore)

hear
hear, where the dry blood talks
　　　where the old appetite walks

　　　　　　　　　la piu saporita et migliore
　　　　　　　　　che si possa truovar al mondo

where it hides, look
in the eye how it runs
in the flesh / chalk

　　　　　but under these petals
　　　　　in the emptiness
　　　　　regard the light, contemplate
　　　　　the flower

whence it arose

　　　　　with what violence benevolence is bought
　　　　　what cost in gesture justice brings
　　　　　what wrongs domestic rights involve
　　　　　what stalks
　　　　　this silence

what pudor pejorocracy affronts
how awe, night-rest and neighborhood can rot
what breeds where dirtiness is law
what crawls
below

III

I am no Greek, hath not th'advantage.
And of course, no Roman:
he can take no risk that matters,
the risk of beauty least of all.

But I have my kin, if for no other reason than
(as he said, next of kin) I commit myself, and,
given my freedom, I'd be a cad
if I didn't. Which is most true.

It works out this way, despite the disadvantage.
I offer, in explanation, a quote:
si j'ai du goût, ce n'est guère
que pour la terre et les pierres

Despite the discrepancy (an ocean   courage   age)
this is also true: if I have any taste
it is only because I have interested myself
in what was slain in the sun

I pose you your question:

shall you uncover honey / where maggots are?

I hunt among stones

11

ABCs

The word forms
on the left: you must
stand in line. Speech
is as swift as synapse
but the acquisition of same
is as long
as I am old

    r a t   on the first floor landing of the three-decker
                    (grey)

    b l a c k   eat a peck of storage batteries 'fore
                    I die

c a b b a g e   my friend Cabbage, with whom to bake potatoes up
                    Fisher's Hill

    r u s t   in the bed of Beaver Brook—from the junk in it

                    And the iris ("flags," we called 'em)

                    And the turtle I was surprised by

up to last night's dream, the long brown body pleased
I kissed her buttock curve

Interiors,
and their registration

Words, form
but the extension of
content

Style, est verbum

The word
is image, and the reverend reverse is
Eliot

Pound
is verse

A B C s (2)

what we do not know of ourselves
of who they are who lie
coiled or unflown
in the marrow of the bone

      one sd:

           of rhythm is image
           of image is knowing
           of knowing there is
           a construct

or to find in a night who it is dwells in that wood where shapes hide
who is this woman or this man whose face we give a name to, whose shoulder
we bite, what landscape
figures ride small horses over, what bloody stumps
these dogs have, how they tear the golden cloak

                          And the boat,

how he swerves it to avoid the yelping rocks
where the tidal river rushes

A B C s   (3—for Rimbaud)

NEWS (o the latest)
& mu-sick, mu-sick—music
worse than war, worse
than peace, & they both dead
And the people's faces
like boils

Who pleas for the heart, for the return of, into the work of,
say, the running of
a street-car?

> Or shall it be rain,
> on a tent   or grass   or birds
> on a wire (5, count 'em, now 3
> on two—or does it come to 1
> on 1? Is it
> Metechevsky?

>> We call it
>> trillings, cleanings,
>> we who want scourings

> Or the watching of, the Passaic of
> orange peels? Cats
> win in urbe, NOT

usura   or those queer long white (like finger bandages
balloons? The dyes
of realism? (Cats,
& industry, not even
violence

15

Why not the brutal, head on?
Fruits? beauty? to want it
so hard? Who
can beat that life
into form, who
is so hopeful—who
has misled us?

To have what back? Is it any more than
a matter of
syllables?

        Yes, mouths bit
        empty air

                They bit. What
                do they bite,
                now? what we needed most
                was something the extension of
                claritas: what do we have
                to report?

THERE WAS A YOUTH
WHOSE NAME WAS THOMAS GRANGER

1

From the beginning, SIN
and the reason, note, known from the start

says Mr. bradford: As it is with waters when
their streames are stopped or damed up, wickednes
(Morton, Morton, Morton)
here by strict laws as in no place more,
or so much, that I have known or heard of,
and ye same more nerly looked unto
(Tom Granger)
so, as it cannot rune in a comone road of liberty
as it would, and is inclined,
it searches every wher (everywhere)
and breaks out wher it getts vente, says he

Rest, Tom, in your pit where they put you
a great & large pitte digged of purposs for them
of Duxbery, servant, being aboute 16. or 17. years of age
his father & mother living at the time at Sityate

espetially drunkennes & unclainnes
incontinencie betweene persons unmaried
but some maried persons allso
And that which is worse
(things fearfull to name)

HAVE BROAK FORTH OFTENER THAN ONCE
IN THIS LAND

2

indicted for yᵉ same) with
a mare, a cowe, tow goats, five sheep, 2. calves
and a turkey (Plymouth Plantation)

Now follows yᵉ ministers answers

3

Mr Charles Channcys   a reverend, godly, very larned man
who shortly thereafter, due to a difference aboute baptising
he holding it ought only to be by diping
that sprinkling was unlawful, removed him selfe
to the same Sityate, a minister to yᵉ church ther

in this case proved, by reference to yᵉ judicials of Moyses
& see: Luthér, Calvin, Hen: Bulin:. Theo: Beza. Zanch:
what greevous sin in yᵉ sight of God,
by yᵉ instigation of burning lusts, set on fire of hell,
to proceede to contactum & fricationem ad emissionem seminis,
        &c.,
& yᵗ contra naturam, or to attempt yᵉ grosse acts of

4

Mr Bradford: I forbear perticulers.
And accordingly he was cast by yᵉ jury,
and condemned.

                    It being demanded of him
the youth confessed he had it of another
who had long used it in old England,
and they kept catle togeather.

18

And after executed about ye 8. of Sept^r, 1642.
A very sade spectakle it was; for first the mare,
and then ye cowe, and ye rest of ye lesser catle,
were kild before his face, according to ye law
Levit: 20.15.

and then he him selfe

and no use made of any part of them

AT YORKTOWN

1

At Yorktown the church
at Yorktown the dead
at Yorktown the grass
are live

       at York-town the earth
piles itself in shallows,
declares itself, like water,
by pools and mounds

2

At Yorktown the dead
are soil
at Yorktown the church
is marl
at Yorktown the swallows
dive where it is greenest,

           the hollows
are eyes are flowers, the heather,
equally accurate, is hands

       at York-town only the flies
dawdle, like history,
in the sun

3

at Yorktown the earthworks
braw
at Yorktown the mortars
of brass, weathered green, of **mermaids**
for handles, of **Latin**
for texts, scream
without noise
like a gull

4

At Yorktown the long dead
loosen the earth, heels
sink in, over an abatis
a bird wheels

and time is a shine caught blue
from a martin's
back

THE PRAISES

She who was burned more than half her body skipped out of death

Observing
that there are five solid figures, the Master
(or so Aetius reports, in the *Placita*)
concluded that
the Sphere of the Universe arose from
the dodecahedron

> whence Alexander,
> appearing in a dream to Antiochus,
> showed him
> And on the morrow, the enemy (the Galates)
> ran before it,
> before the sign, that is

1

By Filius Bonaci, his series, rediscovered Pisa 1202, we shall attack,
for it, too, proceeds asymptotically toward the graphic and tangible, the law
now determined to be
phi

> its capital role in the distribution of
> leaves   seeds   branches on a stem (ex.,
> the ripe sun-flower)
>
> the ratios $\frac{5}{8}$, $\frac{8}{13}$
> in the seed-cones of fir-trees,
> the ratio $\frac{21}{34}$
> in normal daisies

Pendactylism is general in the animal kingdom.
But crystals . . . there, pentagonal forms or lattices
do not, can not appear

So we have it: star and jelly fish, the sea urchin.
And because there is an ideal and constant angle which,
for leaves and branches on a stem, produces
the maximum exposition to light, that light vertical,
fruit blossoms   the briar rose   the passion flower
But lilies   tulips   the hyacinth, like crystals . . .

Here we must stop   And ponder   For nature,
though she is, as you know (so far, that is
as it is allowed to a mortal to know) from all points of view
similar to herself, yet minerals . . .

                    o, that's not fair, let
                    woman keep her jewels, odd man
                    his pleasure of her glow, let
                    your lady Nephritite
                    pumice her malachite, paint
                    her lids green against the light

Sd he:
            to dream takes no effort
                to think is easy
                    to act is more difficult
            but for a man to act after he has taken thought, this!
            is the most difficult thing of all

2

We turn now to Ammonius,
who was present when Nero was,
who is full of delights,
& who smiles quickly

the epiphanies, he says, in this case are four:
1st, to such as begin to learn & to inquire,
the Pythian response,
with flute

(2) when part of the truth is glimpsed, the sun
(a creature of four-fold eyes and heads,
of a ram   a bull   a snake   the bright-eyed lion)
This is little, even though the drum
is added

When a person has got the knowledge, Ammonius
(and he does not mean to be ambiguous)
confers one overwhelming title:
he says a man may then call himself OF THEBES. He may sing

The last, and triumphant mode, I leave, as he leaves it,
untranslated: when men are active, enjoy thought, that is to say
when they talk, they are LESKENOI. They rage

Which is why what is related must remain enigmatic
And why Ammonius excepts, from these epiphanies,
those who are entirely brutish.

Which brings us to what concerns us in the present inquiry.

    Avert, avert, avoid
    pollution, to be clean
    in a dirty time

                O Wheel, aid us
                to get the gurry off

    You would have a sign. Look:
    to fly? a fly can do that;
    to try the moon? a moth
    as well; to walk on water? a straw
    precedes you

                    O Wheel! draw
                    that truth
                    to my house

Like pa does, not like sis,
on all detractors, piss, o advertised earth!
And you, o lady Moon, observe my love,
whence it arose

Whence it arose,
and who it is who sits,
there at the base of the skull, locked
in his throne of bone, that mere pea of bone
where the axes meet, cross-roads of the system
god, converter, discloser, he will answer,
will look out, if you will look, look!

3

What has been lost
is the secret of secrecy, is
the value, viz., that the work get done, and quickly,
without the loss of due and profound respect for
the materials

which is not so easy as it sounds, nor
can it permit the dispersion which follows from
too many having too little
knowledge

                              Says Iamblichus:
        by shipwreck, he perished (Hippasus, that is)
        the first to publish (write down, divulge)
        the secret,
        the construction of, from 12 pentagons,
        the sphere

        "Thus was he punished for his impiety"

                         25

What is necessary is
containment,
that that which has been found out by work may, by work, be passed on
(without due loss of force)
for use
     USE

"And they took over power, political power, in Gr Greece, including
Sicily, and maintained themselves, even after the Master died, until,
at Metapontum, the mob

"Only Philalaos, and Lysis, did not perish in the fire. Later,
Archytas it was, pupil of Philalaos, who, friend to Plato, initiated him,
and, at Tarentum

4

Which is about what we had to say,
the clues, anyhow

What belongs to art and reason is
                         the knowledge of
                                 consequences

L da V, his notebook:

              Every natural action obeys by
              the straightest possible process

IN COLD HELL, IN THICKET

In cold hell, in thicket, how
abstract (as high mind, as not lust, as love is) how
strong (as strut or wing, as polytope, as things are
constellated) how
strung, how cold
can a man stay (can men) confronted
thus?

All things are made bitter, words even
are made to taste like paper, wars get tossed up
like lead soldiers used to be
(in a child's attic) lined up
to be knocked down, as I am,
by firings from a spit-hardened fort, fronted
as we are, here, from where we must go

God, that man, as his acts must, as there is always
a thing he can do, he can raise himself, he raises
on a reed he raises his

Or, if it is me, what
he has to say

1

What has he to say?
In hell it is not easy
to know the traceries, the markings
(the canals, the pits, the mountings by which space

27

declares herself, arched, as she is, the sister,
awkward stars drawn for teats to pleasure him, the brother
who lies in stasis under her, at ease as any monarch or
a happy man

How shall he who is not happy, who has been so made unclear,
who is no longer privileged to be at ease, who, in this brush, stands
reluctant, imageless, unpleasured, caught in a sort of hell, how
shall be convert this underbrush, how turn this unbidden place
how trace and arch again
the necessary goddess?

2

The branches made against the sky are not of use, are
already done, like snow-flakes, do not, cannot service
him who has to raise   (Who puts this on, this damning of his flesh?)
he can, but how far, how sufficiently far can he raise the thickets of
this wilderness?

How can he change, his question is
these black and silvered knivings, these
awkwardnesses?

How can he make these blood-points into panels, into sides
for a king's, for his own
for a wagon, for a sleigh, for the beak of, the running sides of
a vessel fit for
moving?

How can he make out, he asks,
of this low eye-view,
size?

And archings traced and picked enough to hold
to stay, as she does, as he, the brother, when,
here where the mud is, he is frozen, not daring

where the grass grows, to move his feet from fear
he'll trespass on his own dissolving bones, here
where there is altogether too much remembrance?

3

The question, the fear he raises up himself against
(against the same each act is proffered, under the eyes
each fix, the town of the earth over, is managed) is: Who
am I?

Who am I but by a fix, and another,
a particle, and the congery of particles carefully picked one by another,

        as in this thicket, each
        smallest branch, plant, fern, root
        —roots lie, on the surface, as nerves are laid open—
        must now (the bitterness of the taste of her) be
        isolated, observed, picked over, measured, raised
        as though a word, an accuracy were a pincer!
                              this

            is the abstract, this
            is the cold doing, this
            is the almost impossible

So shall you blame those
who give it up, those who say
it isn't worth the struggle?

                    (Prayer
Or a death as going over to—shot by yr own forces—to
a greener place?

                 Neither

any longer
usable)

By fixes only (not even any more by shamans)
can the traceries
be brought out

II

ya, selva oscura, but hell now
is not exterior, is not to be got out of, is
the coat of your own self, the beasts
emblazoned on you   And who
can turn this total thing, invert
and let the ragged sleeves be seen
by any bitch or common character?   Who
can endure it where it is, where the beasts are met,
where yourself is, your beloved is, where she
who is separate from you, is not separate, is not
goddess, is, as your core is,
the making of one hell

where she moves off, where she is
no longer arch

(this is why he of whom we speak does not move, why
he stands so awkward where he is, why
his feet are held, like some ragged crane's
off the nearest next ground, even from
the beauty of the rotting fern his eye
knows, as he looks down, as,
in utmost pain if cold can be so called,
he looks around this battlefield, this
rotted place where men did die, where boys
and immigrants have fallen, where nature
(the years that she's took over)
does not matter, where

that men killed, do kill, that woman kills
is part, too, of his question

30

2

That it is simple, what the difference is—
that a man, men, are now their own wood
and thus their own hell and paradise
that they are, in hell or in happiness, merely
something to be wrought, to be shaped, to be carved, for use, for
others

does not in the least lessen his, this unhappy man's
obscurities, his
confrontations

He shall step, he
will shape, he
is already also
moving off

       into the soil, on to his own bones

he will cross

      (there is always a field,
       for the strong there is always
       an alternative)

              But a field
      is not a choice, is
      as dangerous as a prayer, as a death, as any
      misleading, lady

He will cross

      And is bound to enter (as she is)
      a later wilderness.
              Yet
      what he does here, what he raises up
      (he must, the stakes are such

                                                this at least
is a certainty, this
is a law, is not one of the questions, this
is what was talked of as
—what was it called, demand?)

He will do what he now does, as she will, do
carefully, do
without wavering,
without
              as even the branches,
              even in this dark place, the twigs
                                                how
              even the brow
of what was once to him a beautiful face

as even the snow-flakes waver in the light's eye

              as even forever wavers (gutters
              in the wind of loss)

              even as he will forever waver

              precise as hell is, precise
              as any words, or wagon,
              can be made

THE MOON IS THE NUMBER 18

is a monstrance,
the blue dogs bay,
and the son sits,
grieving

is a grinning god, is
the mouth of, is
the dripping moon

while in the tower the cat
preens
and all motion
is a crab

and there is nothing he can do but what they do, watch
the face of waters, and fire

      The blue dogs paw,
      lick the droppings, dew
      or blood, whatever
      results are. And night,
      the crab, rays round
      attentive as the cat to catch
      human sound

      The blue dogs rue,
      as he does, as he would howl, confronting
      the wind which rocks what was her, while prayers

striate the snow, words blow
as questions cross fast, fast
as flames, as flames form, melt
along any darkness

Birth is an instance as is a host, namely, death

The moon has no air

In the red tower
in that tower where she also sat
in that particular tower where watching & moving are,
there,
there where what triumph there is, is: there
is all substance, all creature
all there is against the dirty moon, against
number, image, sortilege—

alone with cat & crab,
and sound is, is, his
conjecture

TO GERHARDT, THERE, AMONG EUROPE'S
THINGS OF WHICH HE HAS WRITTEN U
IN HIS "BRIEF AN CREELEY UND OLSON

so pawed,
by this long last Bear-son

    with no crockery broken,
    but no smile in my mouth

        June 28th, '51, on this horst
        on the Heat Equator, a mediterranean sea
        to the east, and north
        what saves America from desert, waters
        and thus rain-bearing winds,
        by subsidence, salt-waters
          (by which they came,
          the whelps, looking
          for youth

Which they found.

        And have continuously sought

                  to kill

      (o Old Man,
in winter, when before me, cross my path

in summer, when behind me, cross my path

If you want to shut yourself in, shut yourself in
If you do not want to shut yourself in, come out

> A zoo
> is what he's come to, the old
> Beginner, the old
> Winner

Who took all,
for awhile

> (My grandfather, my grandmother,
> why have you died?
> Did a hand to hand struggle come?
> Did a war, the size of a man's fist come?)

1

The proposition, Gerhardt
is to get it straight, right
from the start.

> Help raise the bones
> of the great man.

> Meat and bones we won't throw away.
> We pile it up in a lonely place.

> We do not throw on the ground.
> Your meat and bones without purpose.
> We take bones and meat.

> O Grandfather,
> you went to war

The first duty is
to knock out his teeth, saying
"These are the teeth with which you devour all animals."

I offer you no proper names
either from great cities
on the other side of civilization
which have only to be visited
to be got the hell out of, by bus
or motorcycle, simply because place
as a force is a lie.
or at most a small truth,
now that man has no oar to screw down into the earth, and say
here i'll plant, does not know
why he should cease
staying on the prowl

                    You climbed up the tree after some foul berry
                    and fell down and died
                    You ate berries, fell from the rock
                    and died
                    You ate sorb berries
                    and died
                    You ate raspberries,
                    drowned in the swamp and died

Or from the other side of time, from a time on the other side of yourself
from which you have so lightly borrowed men, naming them as though,
like your litany of Europe's places, you could take up
their power: magic, my light-fingered faust,
is not so easily sympathetic. Nor are the ladies
worn so decoratively.

                    The top of the spring plant
                    noisily chewing

                    The top of the summer plant
                    noisily chewing

                    On a summer day walk before and behind me
                    on a winter day

37

2

Nor can I talk of method, in the face of your letter,
in verse or otherwise,
as though it were a dance
of rains, or schmerz, of words as signs worn
like a toupee on the head of a Poe cast
in plaster, any method otherwise than
he practised it who gave it up,
after a summer in his mother's barn,
because the place smelled so, because time
his time, precisely this now
And with no back references, no
floating over Asia arrogating
how a raiding party moves in advance of a nation thereby
eventually
giving a language the international power
poets take advantage of. As they also,
with much less reason, from too much economics speak
of the dream
in a peasant's bent shoulders, as though it were true
they cared a damn
for his conversation

> On a mountain with dry stalks, walk
> with a resounding tread
>
> On a mountain with meadow-sweet
> walk with a resounding tread
>
> On the way to your fathers,
> join them

3

Nor of a film, or of strange birds,
or of ordinary ones. Nor with the power of American vocables

would I arm you in Kansas, when you come,
or there, if you have to stay, where you feel so strongly
the dead center of the top of time

                    I am giving you a present

                    I am giving you a present

For you forget (forgetting
is much more your problem
than you know, right-handed one
who so beautifully reminds me
that the birds stand
in the middle of the air
and that always, in that apsed place
in which so many have kneeled
as I do not have the soul to kneel, the fields
are forever harvested, and happy heaven
leans over backwards
to pour its blessings by downfall
on to black earth

Admitting that among the ruins
        with a like schmerz in every vessel of his throat,
        he repeated, "Among the ruins, among them
        the finest memory in the Orient"
one will go about picking up old pieces
        bric-a-brac, he snorted, who did not know whereof he spoke,
        he had so allowed himself to be removed, to back-trail
or put it immediately out of the mind, as some can,
stuff the construction hole quickly with a skyscraper

but you will remember that even Caesar comes to this, certainly you
who has written of Hamlet's death, who is able to handle such large counters
as the classic poet handled bank-notes in our time, before prizes
were his lot, and I am envious, who can do neither

that the point of the rotting of man in his place is also
(beside the long-lived earth of good farmers, its manuring,
what Duncan pointed out America and Russia are very careless with)
what blows about and blocks a hole where the wind was used to go

       (While walking on the earth with stalks
       you received a present

       While walking on the earth with the stalks of plants
       your head was crushed

       You could not see, your eyes got small,
       you could not defecate, you were small
       you could not,
       therefore you died

It is a rod of mountain ash I give you, Rainer Maria Gerhardt,
instead of any other thing, in order that you may also be
left-handed, as he was, your Grandfather,
whom you have all forgotten, have even lost the song of, how
he was to be addressed:

       "Great man,
         in climbing up the tree,
         broke his leg."

I am urging you from here
where nothing is brutal,
not even the old economics
    (I do not dare to breathe
    for what I know the new
    will do) and only the kids kill
frigate-birds, because they have to
to develop a throwing arm

       (as your people knew, if I can lead you
       to go back far enough,
       which is not one step from where you are

"His ear is the earth.
Let you be careful"

that he must be hunted, that to eat
you shall bring him down

"Your head
is the size of a ladle

Your soul
is of the size of a thread

Do not enter my soul by day,
do not enter my dreams by night

that woman—who is, with more resistance
than you seem to have allowed, named—
lends herself to him as concubine

what you forget is, you

are their son! You are not

Telemachus. And that you come back

under your own

steam

There are no broken stones, no statues, no images, phrases, composition
otherwise than
what Creeley and I also have,
and without reference to
what reigned in the house
and is now well dismissed

Let you pray to him, we say
who are without such fatherhood:

"Show your house in spring.

Show a mound of snow in your house in winter.

In summer go in back of and in front of
the children.

Think not badly of the man, go right."

4

Or come here
where we will welcome you
with nothing but what is, with
no useful allusions, with no birds
but those we stone, nothing to eat
but ourselves, no end and no beginning, I assure you, yet
nòt at all primitive, living as we do in a space we do not need to contrive

And with predecessors who, though they are not our nouns, the verbs
are like!

So we are possessed of what you cry over, time
and magic numbers

Language,
my enemie,
is no such system:

"Hey, old man, the war arrived.

Be still, old man.

Your mouth is shut,

your door is shut,"

As I said, I am giving you a present.
To all false dimensions,
including his superb one
who refused to allow the social question in,
to all such fathers and false girls
(one of his, I notice, you take, seriously)
why not say what, somewhere, you must hear the echo of?

                              "One eye
                                sees heaven,
                                another eye
                                sees earth

For the problem is one of focus, of the field as well as the point of
vision: you will solve your problem best
without displacement

                        "One ear
                          hears heaven,
                          another ear
                          hears earth."

In such simplicities I would have you address me,
another time

5

                        The old man, my grandfather, died.
                        The old woman, my grandmother, died.
                        And now my father visits me, clothed
                        in a face he never wore, with an odor
                        I do not know as his, as his was meadow-sweet.
                        He sits, grieving, that she should have worried,
                        and I look up at him as he sits there
                        and if I am his son, this man
                        is from as far a place and time

43

as yours is, carries with him
the strangeness you and I will carry
for our sons, and for like reason,
that we are such that can be pawed

"We are no murderers," they used so carefully to say.

"We have put in order the bones of him
 whom others kill."

You see, we are experienced of what you speak of: silence
with no covering of ashes, geraniums also
and loaded with aphis

of all but war,

but war, too, is dead as the lotus is dead

And our hardness

has been exaggerated. You see,
we see nothing downward: we walk, as your grandfather walked,
without looking at his feet

"And because of meeting the great man,
 a feast is held

Warm yourself,
over the fire of grandfather

This is an offering to the guests, a holiday
of the great man

He will feel satisfied

He will not take revenge

The stick is a reminder, Gerhardt. And the song? what seems
to have been forgotten?

44

Here it is (as we say here, in our anti-cultural speech, made up
of particulars only, which we don't, somehow, confuse with gossip:

> "To his resting place in spring,
>
> to his house in autumn,
>
> I shall go
>
> With autumn plant, arouse the mountain
>
> With spring plant, arouse the mountain
>
> In summer, walk in the background,
> do not frighten the children,
> do not sniff, neither here
> nor there."

LETTER FOR MELVILLE 1951

written to be read AWAY FROM the Melville Society's "One Hundredth Birthday Party" for MOBY-DICK at Williams College, Labor Day Weekend, Sept. 2-4, 1951

MY DEAR ——:

I do thank you, that we hear from you, but the Melville Society invitation came in the same mail with your news of this thing, and do you for a moment think, who have known me 17 years, that I would come near, that I would have anything to do with their business other than to expose it for the promotion it is, than to do my best to make clear who these creatures are who take on themselves to celebrate a spotless book a wicked man once made?

that I find anywhere in my being any excuse for this abomination, for the false & dirty thing which it is—nothing more than a bunch of commercial travellers from the several colleges? Note this incredible copy: "Those who are planning to take part in the English Institute of Columbia University on September 5-8 will find it convenient to attend both conferences"! Can anything be clearer, as to how Melville is being used? And all the other vulgarities of ease and come-on: how pretty the trees are this time of year, how nice of Williams College to take our fifteen bucks, how you won't run over anyone, the conference is so planned—o no let's not run over anyone but him, and just exactly here in the Berkshire hills where he outwrote himself, just where he—when we go together in the sight-seeing bus—where—the house will be open, it has been arranged—he was very clean with his knife, the arrowhead of his attention having struck, there we'll be able to forget he fell in a rut in that very road and had, thereafter, a most bad crick in his back

46

o these
things we can—we must—not speak of, we must avoid *all* of the traffic
except the meals, the sessions, the other points, of interest

for there are most important things
to be taken care of: you see, each of us has families (maybe we have
as many children as he did) and if we don't or we have only a wife
because we really prefer boys, in any case, no matter what the circum-
stances which we will not mention in the speeches (you know that
sort of thing we can only talk about in the halls, outside the meetings,
or, at table, out of the corners of our mouths—you might say, out of
a crack in the grave where a certain sort of barbed ivy has broken in
over the years it has lain and multiplied flat on the rather silly stone
others took some care in placing over the remains—we cannot forget,
even for this instant, that, in order, too, that we can think that we
ourselves are of some present importance, we *have* to—I know, we
really would prefer to be free, *but*—we do have to have an income,
so, you see, you must excuse us if we scratch each other's backs with
a dead man's hand

for after all, who but us, who but us has had the niceness to organize
ourselves in his name, who, outside us, is remembering that this man
a year ago one hundred years ago (you see, we *are* very accurate about
our celebrations, know such things as dates) was, just where we are
gathering just ahead of labor day (walked coldly in a cold & narrow
hall by one window of that hall to the north, into a room, a very
small room also with one window to the same white north) to avoid
the traffic who is, but us, provided with dormitories and catering
services?

Timed in such a way to avoid him, to see
he gets a lot of lip (who hung in a huge jaw)
and no service at all (none of this chicken, he
who is beyond that sort of recall, beyond
any modern highway (which would have saved him
from sciatica? well, that

47

we cannot do for him but we can
we now know so much, we can make clear
how he erred, how, in other ways
—we have made such studies and
we permit ourselves to think—they
allow us to tell each other how wise
he was

He was. Few flying fish
no dolphins and in that glassy sea
two very silly whales throwing
that spout of theirs you might call sibylline
it disappears so fast, why
this year a hundred years ago he
had moved on, was offering
to such as these
a rural bowl of milk, subtitled
the ambiguities

       July
above Sigsbee deep,
the *Lucero del Alba,*
500 tons, 200,000 board feet
of mahogany, the Captain
25, part Negro, part American Indian and perhaps
a little of a certain Cereno, by name
Orestes Camargo
       Herman Melville
looked up again at the weather, noted
that landlessness   And it was not so much truth
as he had thought, even though the ratlines
could still take his weight (185, eyes
blue, hair auburn, a muscular man knowing
that knowledge
is only what makes a ship shape, takes care

48

of the precision of the crossed sign, the feather
and the anchor, the thing
which is not the head but is
where they cross, the edge
the moving edge of force, the wed
of sea and sky (or land & sky), the Egyptian
the American backwards

> (The stern, at evening,
> a place for conversation, to drop paper boats, to ask
> why clouds are painters' business, why now he
> would not write *Moby-Dick*)

Was writing
Pierre: the world
had moved on, in that hallway, moved
north north east, had moved him

> O such fools
> neither of virtue nor of truth
> to associate with
>   to sit to table by
> as once before you, and Harry, and I
> the same table the same Broadhall saw
> water raised by another such to tell us
> this beast hauled up out of great water was
> society!
>
>   this Harvard and this Yale
> as Ossa on Pelion (or,
> as one less than he but
> by that lessness still
> a very great man, said
> of another—who never learned a thing
> from Melville—worth
> "five Oxfords on ten thousand Cambridges"!

o that these fellow diners of yours might know
that poets move very fast, that it is true
it is very wise to stay the hell out of
such traffic, of such labor
which knows no weekend

Please to carry my damnations to each of them
as they sit upon their arse-bones variously
however differently padded, or switching

                    to say please, to them
(whom I would not please any more than he will: he is flying
for the weekend, from Pensacola, where,
any moment, he will dock

please say some very simple things, ask them
to be accurate:
ask one to tell you
what it was like to be a Congregational minister's son Midwest
how hard it was for a boy who liked to read to have to pitch, instead,
hay; and how, now that he has published books, now that he has done that
(even though his edition of this here celebrated man's verse
whom we thought we came here to talk about
has so many carelessnesses in it that, as of this date,
it is quite necessary to do it over)
let him tell you, that no matter how difficult it is
to work in an apartment in a bedroom in a very big city
because the kids are bothersome and have to be locked out, and the wife
is only too good, yet, he did republish enough of this other man
to now have a different professional title, a better salary
and though he wishes he were at Harvard or a Whale,
he is, isn't he, if he is quite accurate, much more liked
by his president?

There'll be main speeches, and one
will do the same thing that other did that other time, tell you
(as he did then who has, since, lost a son in war, society
is such a shambles, such a beast, and altogether not
that white whale), this new one, this new book-maker
will talk about democracy, has such a nose
is so imbued with progress he will classify
the various modes of same (what,
because it was the '30's, and hope was larger, that other
gave us in a broader view) but press him, ask him
is it not true you have, instead, made all this make your way
into several little magazines however old they are?

                             (How much light
        the black & white man threw—Orestes!—on
        democracy!)

        as, if you were on the floor that night, you could see
        just what are the differences of the hidden rears
        of each of your fellow celebrators

Myself, I'd like to extricate you who have the blood of him, and another
who loves him as a doctor knows
a family doctor, how
his mother stayed inside him, how
the compact came out hate, and what
this kept him from, despite
how far he travelled

        (The match-box, with a match for mast,
        goes backward gaily, bumping
        along the wake)

What they'll forget—they'll smother you—is
there is only one society, there is no other than

51

how many we do not know, where
and why they read a book, and that
the reading of a book can save a life, they
do not come to banquets, and Nathaniel Hawthorne
whom Herman Melville loved
will not come, nor Raymond Weaver
who loved them both because they loved each other.

You have the right to be there
because you loved an old man's walk
and took a little attic box, and books.
And there is he, the doctor, whom I love
and by his presence side by side with you
will speak for Melville and myself, he
who was himself saved, who
because, in the middle of the Atlantic,
an appendectomy was called for, read
a sea story once, and since
has gone by the pole-star, a scalpel overside
for rudder, has moved on from Calypso, huge
in the despatch of
the quick-silver god

Yet I wish so very much that neither of you mixed
(as Leyda hasn't) in this middle place, in such salad
as these caterers will serve!

For you will have to hear one very bright man speak, so bright
he'll sound so good that every one of you will think
he knows whereof he speaks, he'll say such forward things, he'll tag
the deific principle in nature, the heroic
principle in man, he'll spell
what you who do not have such time to read as he
such definitions so denotatively clear you'll think you'll understand
(discourse is such a lie) that Herman Melville
was no professional, could not accomplish

such mentality and so, as amateur (as this clear neuter will make clear)
was anguished all his life in struggle, not with himself, he'll say,
no, not with when
shall i eat my lunch Elizabeth has set outside the door so quiet
it was not even a mouse, my prose today
is likewise, the cows, what a damned nuisance they also are, why
do i continue to extend my language horizontally when
i damn well know what is
a water-spout

No, he'll skillfully confuse you, he knows such words
as mythic, such adjectives that fall so easily you'll think it's true
Melville was a risky but creative mingling
                    (how they put words on, that this lad was so
who stowed himself with roaches and a blue-shining corpse at age 16: "Hey!
Jackson!"

                    the diced bones—now this too, he
                    who is also of the one society
                    who likewise lifted altars
                    too high (a typewriter
                    in a tree) and spilled himself
                    into the honey-head, died
                    the blond ant
                    so pleasantly

                              as though he did not want to woo
                              to chance a Bronx grave, preferred
                              to choose his own headland

All these that you will sit with—"a mingling," he will drone on,
"of the fortunate and the injurious"

                    And only you, and Harry (who knows)
                    will not be envious, will know
                    that he knows not one thing
                    this brightest of these mischievous men

who does not know that it is not the point
either of the hook or the plume which lies
cut on this brave man's grave
—on all of us—
but that where they cross is motion,
where they constantly moving cross anew, cut
this new instant open—as he is who
is this weekend in his old place
presumed on

                                I tell you,

he'll look on you all with an eye you have the color of.

He'll not say a word because he need not, he said so many.

ANECDOTES OF THE LATE WAR

1.

the lethargic vs violence as alternatives of each other for los americanos
       & U S Grant (at Shiloh, as ex.) had the gall to stay
       inside a lethargy until it let him down into either
       vice (Galena, or, as president) or
       a virtue of such a movement as, example,
       Vicksburg

       say that he struck, going down, either
       morass or
       rock—and when it was rock, he was

— this wld seem to be the power in the principle —

able to comprehend the movement of mass of men, the
transposition of the
Mississippi (Or
continents, example,
somebody else than:
grant

       better, that is, that a man stay lethargic than
blow somebody's face off — off,
the face of, blow
the earth

2.

that (like the man sd) Booth
killing Lincoln is the melodrama right with
the drama: Mister Christ and
Broadway

          Or going out to Bull Run looking for
Waterloo. the
diorama. And having to get the fastidious hell home
that afternoon
as fast as the carriage horses
can't make it (Lee Highway
littered with broken
elegances

          Reverse of
sic transit gloria, the
Latin American whom the cab driver told me
he picked up at Union Station had
one word of english—link-
cone. And drove him
straight to the monument, the man
went up the stairs and fell down on his knees
where he could see the statue and stayed there
in the attitude of prayer

3.
whoop,
went the bird
in the tree the day
the fellow
fell down
in the thicket

whoop, was the bird's
lay as the fellow lay

and I picked up a minie ball
(the way
it can be
again
of an afternoon,

56

or with the French girl Brandy Station
was
thick grass
and the gray house and back of it

yes   mam   the   movement
of horses, as
—I repeat—
the bird.

4.

West Point is wasn't. Nor New England. Nor
those cavalry
flauntlets

> As the Mexican War was
> filibusterers
> in the West,
> and cadets
> before Chapultepec: the elevator
>
> goink down
> from waterloo,
> the Civil War

was the basement. Only nobody
except butternut
and his fellow on the other side
wanted to believe it, they all wanted

what Jay Gould got

(and Joe Blow got swap
in the side of the head

5.

Now you take this Forrest, Nathan Bedford Forrest. He stalks the Western theater of operations as something the English, to this day, think Lee wouldn't have surpassed had anybody dared to give this Memphis slave-trader the width of men and field to command which he only had as first Grand Wizard of the Ku Klux Klan. And didn't use, Forrest could already avoid the temptation of the Filibusterer, he had applied first principles in the War.

What I'd wanted to say was,
that he's a man so locked in the act of himself

> (right up to after Davis had been taken
> and no last movie scene to the way he was still
> cutting tracks behind U. S. Army units, a very

exact and busy man.

I also have to voice this impression of him to give, if it does, the sense of how he was:

> he's like a man his tongue was cut out,
> before even Shiloh showed him
> an extraordinary executive
> of men horses and goods

6.

Two things still aren't brought in to give context to the War: (1), that you don't get Grant except as you find what he was that Geo Washington also comes alive at only if you realize he was to real estate—

> and I mean land
when land was as oil steel and what, now?

Managing men, wasn't it, when men suddenly what was Grant's

58

because of the industrial revolution

were what the guys who died then were

                              For the first time,
like that, the sprawled fellow Devil's Glen, natural
resource.

        The other half of it—(2)—that each one of them,

Butternut,

and Yankee Doodle,

weren't as different as North and South, farmer and factory etc.

They were — for the first time — enough of them.

                              Plus railroad tracks
                              to be moved around as
utility

        The leaders,   Grant Sherman Forrest not
                                Jeb Stuart
        and themselves

        the birth of

        the recent   And Lincoln

        likewise   (after Christ

        Link-cone

7.

You take it
from there

8.

What he said was, in that instance
I got there first
with the most men

Grant didn't hurry.
He just had the most.

More of the latter died.

the dross of verse. Rhyme!
when iron (steel)
has expelled Confucius
from China. Pittsburgh!
beware: the Master
bewrays his vertu.
To clank like you do
he brings coolie verse
to teach you equity,
who layed down such rails!

Who doesn't know a whorehouse
from a palace (who doesn't know the Bowery
is still the Bowery, even if it is winos
who look like a cold wind, put out their hands
to keep up their pants

        that the willow or the peach blossom
        ...Whistler, be with America
        at this hour

        open galleries. And sell
        Chinese prints, at the opening,
        even let the old ladies in—

        let decoration thrive, when
        clank is let back
        into your song

                    when voluntarism
              abandons
              poetic means

Noise! that Confucius himself
should try to alter it, he
who taught us all
that no line must sleep,
that as the line goes so goes
the Nation! that the Master
should now be embraced by the demon
he drove off!   O Ruler

          in the time of chow,
          that the Soldier
          should lose the Battle!

          that what the eye sees,
          that in the East the sun untangles itself
          from among branches,
          should be made to sound as though there were still roads
          on which men hustled
          to get to paradise, to get to
          Bremerton
          shipyards!

          II

that the great 'ear
can no longer 'hear!

                o Whitman,
                let us keep our trade with you when
                the Distributor
                who couldn't go beyond wood,
                apparently,
                has gone out of business

                                    62

let us not wear shoddy
mashed out of
even the Master's
old clothes, let us bite off Father's
where the wool's
got too long (o Solomon Levi

    in your store on Salem Street,
     we'll go there to buy our ulsterettes,
    and everything else that's neat

III

We'll to these woods
no more, where we were used
to get so much, (Old Bones
do not try to dance

    go still
    now that your legs

       the Charleston
       is still for us

         You can watch

It is too late
to try to teach us

     we are the process

      and our feet

        We do not march

We still look

   And see

     what we see

        We do not see
        ballads

other than our own.

63

THE DEATH OF EUROPE

(a funeral poem for Rainer M. Gerhardt)

Rainer,
the man who was about to celebrate his 52nd birthday
the day I learned of your death at 28, said:
"I lie out on Dionysius' tongue"!

the sort of language you talked, and I did,
correctly —
            as I heard this other German wrongly,
from his accent, and because I was thinking of you,
talking of how much you gave us all hearing
in Germany (as I watch a salamander on the end of a dead pine branch
snagging flies), what I heard this man almost twice your age say was,
"I lie out on a dinosaur's tongue"!

for my sense, still, is that,
despite your sophistication
and your immense labors . . .

It will take some telling. It has to do with what WCW
(of all that you published in *fragmente,* to see Bill's
R R BUMS in futura!

                    it has to do with how far back are

Americans,
as well as,
Germans

"walk on spongey feet
if you would cross

carry purslane
if you get into her bed

guard the changes
when you scratch your ear

I

It is this business
that you should die!
Who shot up,
out of the ruins,
and hung there,
in the sky,
the first of Europe
I could have words with:

as Holderlin on Patmos you
trying to hold bay leaves
on a cinder block!

Now I can only console you,
sing of willows,
and dead branches,
worry the meanness '
that you do not live,
wear the ashes
of loss

Neither of us
carrying a stick
any more

Creeley told me
how you lived

II

I have urged anyone
back (as Williams asked
that Sam Houston
be recognized
                as I said,
Rainer, plant
your ash

      "I drive a stake into the ground, isn't it silly,"
I said out loud in the night, "to drive a stake into the ground?"

How primitive
does one have to get? Or,

as you and I were both open
to the charge: how large

can a quote

get, he

said, eyeing me

with a blue

eye

            Were your eyes

            brown, Rainer?

            Rainer,

            who is in the ground,

            what did you look like?

66

Did you die of your head bursting

like a land-mine?

Did you walk

on your own unplanted self?

III

It is not hell you came into,
or came out of. It is not moly
any of us are given. It is merely
that we are possessed of
the irascible. We are blind
not from the darkness
but by creation we are
moles. We are let out
sightless, and thus miss
what we are given, what woman
is, what your two sons
looking out of a picture at me,
sitting on some small hillside —

they have brown eyes, surely.

Rainer, the thyrsus
is down

I can no longer
put anything
into your hands

It does no good
for me to wish
to arm you

I can only carry laurel,
and some red flowers,
mere memorials, not cut

with my own knife an oar
for you, last poet
of a civilization

You are nowhere
but in the ground

IV

What breaks my heart
is that your grandfather
did not do better, that our grandmothers
(I think we agreed)
did not tell us
the proper tales

so that we are as raw
as our inventions, have not the teeth
to bite off Grandfather's
paws

(O, Rainer,
you should have ridden your bike
across the Atlantic instead of your mind,
that bothered itself too much
with how we were hanging on
to the horse's tail, fared, fared
we who had Sam Houston, not
Ulysses

I can only cry: Those
who gave you not enough
caused you to settle for
too little

The ground
is now the sky

68

v

But even Bill
is not protected,
no swift messenger
puts pussley
even in his hand,
open,

as it is, no one says how
to eat
at the hairy table

         (as your scalp
also lifted,
         as your ears
did not stay
silk

         O my collapsed brother,
         the body
         does bring us
         down
             The images
         have to be
         contradicted
               The metamorphoses
         are to be
         undone

         The stick,
         and the ear

         are to be no more than

         they are: the cedar

         and the lebanon

of this impossible

life.

I give you no visit

to your mother.

What you have left us

is what you did

It is enough

It is what we

praise

I take back

the stick.

I open my hand

to throw dirt

into your grave

I praise you

who watched the riding

on the horse's back

It was your glory to know

that we must mount

O that the Earth

had to be given to you

this way!

O Rainer, rest

in the false

peace

Let us who live

try

A NEWLY DISCOVERED 'HOMERIC' HYMN

(for Jane Harrison, if she were alive)

Hail and beware the dead who will talk life until you are blue
in the face. And you will not understand what is wrong,
they will not be blue, they will have tears in their eyes,
they will seem to you so much more full of life
than the rest of us, and they will ask so much, not of you no
but of life, they will cry, isn't it this way, if it isn't
I don't care for it, and you will feel the blackmail, you will not know
what to answer, it will all have become one mass

Hail and beware them, for they come from where you have not been,
they come from where you cannot have come, they come into life
by a different gate. They come from a place which is not easily known,
it is known only to those who have died. They carry seeds
you must not touch, you must not touch the pot they taste of,
no one must touch the pot, no one must, in their season.

Hail and beware them, in their season. Take care. Prepare
to receive them, they carry what the living cannot do without,
but take the proper precautions, do the prescribed things, let
down the thread from the right shoulder. And from the forehead.
And listen to what they say, listen to the talk, hear
every word of it — they are drunk from the pot, they speak
like no living man may speak, they have the seeds in their mouth —
listen, and beware

Hail them solely that they have the seeds in their mouth, they
are drunk, you cannot do without a drunkenness, seeds can't,
they must be soaked in the contents of the pot, they must be all one mass.
But you who live cannot know what else the seeds must be. Hail
and beware the earth, where the dead come from. Life
is not of the earth. The dead are of the earth. Hail and beware
the earth, where the pot is buried.

Greet the dead in the dead man's time. He is drunk of the pot.
He speaks like spring does. He will deceive you. You are meant
to be deceived. You must observe the drunkenness. You are not to
drink. But you must hear, and see. You must beware.

Hail them, and fall off. Fall off! The drink is not yours,
it is not yours! You do not come
from the same place, you do not suffer as the dead do,
they do not suffer, they need, because they have drunk of the pot,
they need. Do not drink of the pot, do not touch it. Do not touch
them.

   Beware the dead. And hail them. They teach you drunkenness.
You have your own place to drink. Hail and beware them, when they come.

AS THE DEAD PREY UPON US

As the dead prey upon us,
they are the dead in ourselves,
awake, my sleeping ones, I cry out to you,
disentangle the nets of being!

I pushed my car, it had been sitting so long unused.
I thought the tires looked as though they only needed air.
But suddenly the huge underbody was above me, and the rear tires
were masses of rubber and thread variously clinging together

as were the dead souls in the living room, gathered
about my mother, some of them taking care to pass
beneath the beam of the movie projector, some record
playing on the victrola, and all of them
desperate with the tawdriness of their life in hell

I turned to the young man on my right and asked, "How is it,
there?" And he begged me protestingly don't ask, we are poor
poor. And the whole room was suddenly posters and presentations
of brake linings and other automotive accessories, cardboard
displays, the dead roaming from one to another
as bored back in life as they are in hell, poor and doomed
to mere equipments

                my mother, as alive as ever she was, asleep
when I entered the house as I often found her in a rocker
under the lamp, and awaking, as I came up to her, as she ever had

I found out she returns to the house once a week, and with her
the throng of the unknown young who center on her as much in death
as other like suited and dressed people did in life

O the dead!

        and the Indian woman and I
        enabled the blue deer
        to walk

        and the blue deer talked,
        in the next room,
        a Negro talk

        it was like walking a jackass,
        and its talk
        was the pressing gabber of gammers
        of old women

        and we helped walk it around the room
        because it was seeking socks
        or shoes for its hooves
        now that it was acquiring

        human possibilities

In the five hindrances men and angels
stay caught in the net, in the immense nets
which spread out across each plane of being, the multiple nets
which hamper at each step of the ladders as the angels
and the demons
and men
go up and down

        Walk the jackass
        Hear the victrola
        Let the automobile

75

          be tucked into a corner of the white fence
          when it is a white chair. Purity

is only an instant of being, the trammels

recur

In the five hindrances, perfection
is hidden
                    I shall get
                    to the place
                    10 minutes late.

                    It will be 20 minutes
                    of 9. And I don't know,

                    without the car,

                    how I shall get there

 O peace, my mother, I do not know
how differently I could have done
what I did or did not do.

                    That you are back each week
                    that you fall asleep
                    with your face to the right

                    that you are as present there
                    when I come in as you were
                    when you were alive

                    that you are as solid, and your flesh
                    is as I knew it, that you have the company
                    I am used to your having

but o, that you all find it
such a cheapness!

o peace, mother, for the mammothness
of the comings and goings
of the ladders of life

The nets we are entangled in. Awake,
my soul, let the power into the last wrinkle
of being, let none of the threads and rubber of the tires
be left upon the earth. Let even your mother
go. Let there be only paradise

The desperateness is, that the instant
which is also paradise (paradise
is happiness) dissolves
into the next instant, and power
flows to meet the next occurrence

        Is it any wonder
        my mother comes back?
        Do not that throng
        rightly seek the room
        where they might expect
        happiness? They did not complain
        of life, they obviously wanted
        the movie, each other, merely to pass
        among each other there,
        where the real is, even to the display cards,
        to be out of hell

        The poverty
        of hell

O souls, in life and in death,
awake, even as you sleep, even in sleep
know what wind

even under the crankcase of the ugly automobile
lifts it away, clears the sodden weights of goods,
equipment, entertainment, the foods the Indian woman,
the filthy blue deer, the 4 by 3 foot 'Viewbook,'
the heaviness of the old house, the stuffed inner room
lifts the sodden nets

        and they disappear as ghosts do,
        as spider webs, nothing
        before the hand of man

        The vent! You must have the vent,
        or you shall die. Which means
        never to die, the ghastliness

        of going, and forever
        coming back, returning
        to the instants which were not lived

        O mother, this I could not have done,
        I could not have lived what you didn't,
        I am myself netted in my own being

        I want to die. I want to make that instant, too,
        perfect

        O my soul, slip
        the cog

    II

The death in life (death itself)
is endless, eternity
is the false cause

The knot is other wise, each topological corner
presents itself, and no sword
cuts it, each knot is itself its fire

each knot of which the net is made
is for the hands to untake
and knot's making. And touch alone

can turn the knot into its own flame

        (o mother, if you had once touched me

         o mother, if I had once touched you)

The car did not burn. Its underside
was not presented to me
a grotesque corpse. The old man

merely removed it as I looked up at it,
and put it in a corner of the picket fence
like was it my mother's white dog?

or a child's chair

        The woman,
        playing on the grass,
        with her son (the woman next door)

        was angry with me whatever it was
        slipped across the playpen or whatever
        she had out there on the grass

        And I was quite flip in reply
        that anyone who used plastic
        had to expect things to skid

        and break, that I couldn't worry
        that her son might have been hurt
        by whatever it was I sent skidding

        down on them.

It was just then I went into my house
and to my utter astonishment
found my mother sitting there

as she always had sat, as must she always
forever sit there her head lolling
into sleep? Awake, awake my mother

what wind will lift you too
forever from the tawdriness,
make you rich as all those souls

crave crave crave

to be rich?

They are right. We must have
what we want. We cannot afford
not to. We have only one course:

the nets which entangle us are flames

        O souls, burn
        alive, burn now

        that you may forever
        have peace, have

        what you crave

        O souls,
        go into everything,
        let not one knot pass
        through your fingers

        let not any they tell you
        you must sleep as the net
        comes through your authentic hands

What passes
is what is, what shall be, what has
been, what hell and heaven is
is earth to be rent, to shoot you
through the screen of flame which each knot
hides as all knots are a wall ready
to be shot open by you

                              the nets of being
are only eternal if you sleep as your hands
ought to be busy. Method, method

I too call on you to come
to the aid of all men, to women most
who know most, to woman to tell
men to awake. Awake, men,
awake

I ask my mother
to sleep. I ask her
to stay in the chair.
My chair
is in the corner of the fence.
She sits by the fireplace made of paving stones. The blue deer
need not trouble either of us.

And if she sits in happiness the souls
who trouble her and me
will also rest. The automobile

has been hauled away.

THE LORDLY AND ISOLATE SATYRS

The lordly and isolate Satyrs — look at them come in
on the left side of the beach
like a motorcycle club! And the handsomest of them,
the one who has a woman, driving that snazzy
convertible

        Wow, did you ever see even in a museum
such a collection of boddisatvahs, the way
they come up to their stop, each of them
as though it was a rudder
the way they have to sit above it
and come to a stop on it, the monumental solidity
of themselves, the Easter Island
they make of the beach, the Red-headed Men

        These are the Androgynes,
the Fathers behind the father, the Great Halves

Or as that one was, inside his pants, the Yiddish poet
a vegetarian. Or another — all in his mouth — a snarl
of the Sources. Or the one I loved most, who once,
once only, let go the pain, the night he got drunk,
and I put him to bed, and he said, Bad blood.

        Or the one who cracks and doesn't know
that what he thinks are a thousand questions are suddenly
a thousand lumps thrown up where the cloaca
again has burst: one looks into the face and exactly as suddenly
it isn't the large eyes and nose but the ridiculously small mouth
which you are looking down as one end of

        — as the Snarled Man

is a monocyte.

Hail the ambiguous Fathers, and look closely
at them, they are the unadmitted, the club of Themselves,
weary riders, but who sit upon the landscape as the Great
Stones. And only have fun among themselves. They are
the lonely ones

Hail them, and watch out. The rest of us,
on the beach as we had previously known it, did not know
there was this left side. As they came riding in from the sea
— we did not notice them until they were already creating
the beach we had not known was there — but we assume
they came in from the sea. We assume that. We don't know.

In any case the whole sea was now a hemisphere,
and our eyes like half a fly's, we saw twice as much. Everything opened, even if the newcomers just sat, didn't,
for an instant, pay us any attention. We were as we had been,
in that respect. We were as usual, the children were being fed pop
and potato chips, and everyone was sprawled as people are
on a beach. Something had happened but the change
wasn't at all evident. A few drops of rain
would have made more of a disturbance.

There we were. They, in occupation of the whole view
in front of us and off to the left where we were not used to look.
And we, watching them pant from their exertions, and talk to each other,
the one in the convertible the only one who seemed to be circulating.
And he was dressed in magnificent clothes, and the woman with him
a dazzling blond, the new dye making her hair a delicious
streaked ash. She was as distant as the others. She sat in her flesh too.

These are our counterparts, the unknown ones.

They are here. We do not look upon them as invaders. Dimensionally

they are larger than we — all but the woman. But we are not suddenly

small. We are as we are. We don't even move, on the beach.

It is a stasis. Across nothing at all we stare at them.
We can see what they are. They don't notice us. They have merely
and suddenly moved in. They occupy our view. They are between us
and the ocean. And they have given us a whole new half of beach.

As of this moment, there is nothing else to report.
It is Easter Island transplanted to us. With the sun, and a warm
summer day, and sails out on the harbor they're here, the Con-
temporaries. They have come in.

Except for the stirring of the leader, they are still
catching their breath. They are almost like scooters the way
they sit there, up a little, on their thing. It is as though
the extra effort of it tired them the most. Yet that just there
was where their weight and separateness — their immensities —
lay. Why they seem like boddisatvahs. The only thing one noticed
is the way their face breaks when they call across to each other.
Or actually speak quite quietly, not wasting breath. But the face
loses all containment, they are fifteen year old boys at the moment
they speak to each other. They are not gods. They are not even stone.
They are doubles. They are only Source. When they act like us
they go to pieces. One notices then that their skin
is only creased like red-neck farmers. And that they are all
freckled. The red-headed people have the hardest time
to possess themselves. Is it because they were over-
fired? Or why — even to their beautiful women — do the red ones
have only that half of the weight?

We look at them, and begin to know. We begin to see
who they are. We see why they are satyrs, and why one half
of the beach was unknown to us. And now that it is known,
now that the beach goes all the way to the headland we thought
we were huddling ourselves up against, it turns out it is the
same. It is beach. The Visitors — Resters — who, by being there,
made manifest what we had not known — that the beach fronted wholly
to the sea — have only done that, completed the beach.

                              The difference is
we are more on it. The beauty of the white of the sun's light, the
blue the water is, and the sky, the movement on the painted landscape, the boy-town the scene was, is now pierced with angels and
with fire. And winter's ice shall be as brilliant in its time as
life truly is, as Nature is only the offerer, and it is we
who look to see what the beauty is.

                              These visitors, now stirring
to advance, to go on wherever they do go restlessly never completing
their tour, going off on their motorcycles, each alone except for
the handsome one, isolate huge creatures wearing down nothing as
they go, their huge third leg like carborundum, only the vault
of their being taking rest, the awkward boddhas

                              We stay. And watch them
gather themselves up. We have no feeling except love. They are not
ours. They are of another name. These are what the gods are. They
look like us. They are only in all parts larger. But the size is
only different. The difference is, they are not here, they are not
on this beach in this sun which, tomorrow, when we come to swim,
will be another summer day. They can't talk to us. We have no desire
to stop them any more than, as they made their camp, only possibly
the woman in the convertible one might have wanted to be familiar
with. The Leader was too much as they.

                              They go. And the day

85

VARIATIONS DONE FOR GERALD VAN DE WIELE

I. LE BONHEUR

dogwood flakes
what is green

the petals
from the apple
blow on the road

mourning doves
mark the sway
of the afternoon, bees
dig the plum blossoms

the morning
stands up straight, the night
is blue from the full of the April moon

iris and lilac, birds
birds, yellow flowers
white flowers, the Diesel
does not let up dragging
the plow

          as the whippoorwill,
the night's tractor, grinds
his song

and no other birds but us
are as busy (O saisons, o chateaux!

Délires!
                    What soul
is without fault?

Nobody studies
happiness

Every time the cock crows
I salute him

I have no longer any excuse
for envy. My life

has been given its orders: the seasons
seize

the soul and the body, and make mock
of any dispersed effort. The hour of death

is the only trespass

II. THE CHARGE

dogwood flakes
the green

the petals from the apple-trees
fall for the feet to walk on

the birds are so many they are
loud, in the afternoon

they distract, as so many bees do
suddenly all over the place

87

With spring one knows today to see
that in the morning each thing

is separate but by noon
they have melted into each other

and by night only crazy things
like the full moon and the whippoorwill

and us, are busy. We are busy
if we can get by that whiskered bird,

that nightjar, and get across, the moon
is our conversation, she will say

what soul
isn't in default?

can you afford not to make
the magical study

which happiness is? do you hear
the cock when he crows? do you know the charge,

that you shall have no envy, that your life
has its orders, that the seasons

seize you too, that no body and soul are one
if they are not wrought

in this retort? that otherwise efforts
are efforts? And that the hour of your flight

will be the hour of your death?

III. SPRING

The dogwood
lights up the day.

The April moon
flakes the night.

Birds, suddenly,
are a multitude

The flowers are ravined
by bees, the fruit blossoms

are thrown to the ground, the wind
the rain forces everything. Noise —

even the night is drummed
by whippoorwills, and we get

as busy, we plow, we move,
we break out, we love. The secret

which got lost neither hides
nor reveals itself, it shows forth

tokens. And we rush
to catch up. The body

whips the soul. In its great desire
it demands the elixir

In the roar of spring,
transmutations. Envy

drags herself off. The fault of the body and the soul
— that they are not one —

the matutinal cock clangs
and singleness: we salute you

season of no bungling

THE LIBRARIAN

The landscape (the landscape!) again: Gloucester,
the shore one of me is (duplicates), and from which
(from offshore, I, Maximus) am removed, observe.

In this night I moved on the territory with combinations
(new mixtures) of old and known personages: the leader,
my father, in an old guise, here selling books and manuscripts.

My thought was, as I looked in the window of his shop,
there should be materials here for Maximus, when, then,
I saw he was the young musician has been there (been before me)

before. It turned out it wasn't a shop, it was a loft (wharf-
house) in which, as he walked me around, a year ago
came back (I had been there before, with my wife and son,

I didn't remember, he presented me insinuations via
himself and his girl) both of whom I had known for years.
But never in Gloucester. I had moved them in, to my country.

His previous appearance had been in my parents' bedroom where I
found him intimate with my former wife: this boy
was now the Librarian of Gloucester, Massachusetts!

> Black space,
> old fish-house.
> Motions
> of ghosts.
> I,
> dogging
> his steps.

He
(not my father,
by name himself
with his face
twisted
at birth)
possessed of knowledge
pretentious
giving me
what in the instant
I knew better of.

But the somber
place, the flooring
crude like a wharf's
and a barn's
space

I was struck by the fact I was in Gloucester, and that my daughter
was there — that I would see her! She was over the Cut. I
hadn't even connected her with my being there, that she was

here. That she was there (in the Promised Land — the Cut!
But there was this business, of poets, that all my Jews
were in the fish-house too, that the Librarian had made a party

I was to read. They were. There were many of them, slumped
around. It was not for me. I was outside. It was the Fort.
The Fort was in East Gloucester — old Gorton's Wharf, where the Library

was. It was a region of coal houses, bins. In one a gang
was beating someone to death, in a corner of the labyrinth
of fences. I could see their arms and shoulders whacking

down. But not the victim. I got out of there. But cops
tailed me along the Fort beach toward the Tavern

The places still
half-dark, mud,
coal-dust.

There is no light
east
of the Bridge

Only on the headland
toward the harbor
from Cressy's

have I seen it (once
when my daughter ran
out on a spit of sand

isn't even there.) Where
is Bristow? when does I-A
get me home? I am caught

in Gloucester. (What's buried
behind Lufkin's
Diner? Who is

Frank Moore?

MOONSET, GLOUCESTER, DECEMBER 1, 1957, 1:58 AM

Goodbye red moon
In that color you set
west of the Cut I should imagine
forever Mother

After 47 years this month
a Monday at 9 AM
you set I rise I hope
a free thing as probably
what you more were Not
the suffering one you sold
sowed me on Rise
Mother from off me
God damn you God damn me my
misunderstanding of you

I can die now I just begun to live

THE DISTANCES

So the distances are Galatea
                              and one does fall in love and desires
mastery

            old Zeus — young Augustus

Love knows no distance, no place
                              is that far away or heat changes
into signals, and control

            old Zeus — young Augustus

Death is a loving matter, then, a horror
                              we cannot bide, and avoid
by greedy life

            we think all living things are precious
            — Pygmalions

                              a German inventor in Key West
who had a Cuban girl, and kept her, after her death
in his bed
                              after her family retrieved her
he stole the body again from the vault

Torso on torso in either direction,
            young Augustus

                              out via nothing where messages
are

94

          or in, down La Cluny's steps to the old man sitting
a god throned on torsoes,

                    old Zeus

Sons go there hopefully as though there was a secret, the object
to undo distance?
                              They huddle there, at the bottom
of the shaft, against one young bum
                              or two loving cheeks,
               Augustus?

You can teach the young nothing
                              all of them go away, Aphrodite
tricks it out,
               old Zeus—young Augustus

You have love, and no object
                    or you have all pressed to your nose
which is too close,
               old Zeus hiding in your chin your young
               Galatea

the girl who makes you weep, and you keep the corpse live by all
your arts
               whose cheek do you stroke when you stroke the stone face
               of young Augustus, made for bed in a military camp,
               o Caesar?

O love who places all where each is, as they are, for every moment,
yield
               to this man
                         that the impossible distance
be healed,

that young Augustus
and old Zeus
be enclosed

"I wake you,
stone. Love this man."